First School Dictionary Skills

Barry and
Anita Scholes

Collins

Collins First School Dictionary Skills

First published 2001

10 9 8 7 6 5 4 3 2

ISBN 0 00 711992 5

A catalogue record for this book is available from the British Library.

Published by HarperCollins*Publishers* Ltd
77-85 Fulham Palace Road
Hammersmith
London W6 8JB

Telephone ordering and information
0870 0100 441

Author: Barry and Anita Scholes
Editor: Mitzi Bales
Cover designer: Susi Martin
Design: Grasshopper Design Company
Illustrator: Stephanie Strickland

Printed in Great Britain by Martins the Printers, Berwick

Contents

Introduction

Collins Dictionary Skills

Collins Dictionary Skills provide all-in-one support for developing dictionary skills. Each Skills book provides:

- photocopiable activity sheets, differentiated for a wide range of abilities
- clear teaching notes and answers
- lesson planning charts that match each activity to National Literacy Strategy objectives and Scottish 5–14 Guidelines.

For maximum support, use each **Collins Dictionary Skills** book with its matching Collins Children's Dictionary.

Collins Dictionaries – for children aged 2 to 11+

Developed in consultation with teachers, children's lexicographers, educational advisors and literacy, numeracy and science specialists, these clear, colourful dictionaries have been written and designed to support today's Primary classroom requirements.

Collins Children's Dictionaries are carefully streamlined to provide a dictionary for each key level of literacy development. Because Collins' range of dictionaries progressively builds skills, children will be able to move confidently between levels and become independent dictionary users.

Children need to acquire the ability to use a dictionary successfully and independently. Collins Children's Dictionaries have been designed to provide all the support that children need, by means of:

- clear, easy-to-use design
- child-oriented definitions and examples
- progressive building of key skills as children move from level to level.

The Collins Children's Dictionary range:

- *builds essential dictionary skills* progressively, step by step, from beginner to advanced
- supports *today's curriculum needs* from the Early Learning Goals to SATs
- incorporates special features to *encourage independent learning*, such as annotated introductions, theme pages, grammar help, word banks and word histories
- has been *rigorously researched and trialled* with teachers and pupils
- has been compiled by a team of experts.

About *Collins First School Dictionary*

Collins First School Dictionary is designed for children aged 5 and over. It is full of helpful and educationally sound features, including:

- **Colour headwords** and **guidewords**, plus an **alphabet line** on every page for easy reference.
- **Big letters** at the top of each page for each new letter.
- Clear, child-friendly **definitions**. These are numbered if there is more than one meaning.
- **Example sentences** showing the headword used in context.
- **Illustrations** to help the user read the word and understand its meaning.
- **Plurals** of nouns, **tenses** of verbs and **comparative forms** of adjectives with their appropriate headword.
- Where to look for **more information**. Some definitions tell the user to look at another headword or at the pages at the back of the dictionary for further information.

Other features

- **Topic pages** at the back of the dictionary. These support children's writing while helping to build vocabulary. They include labelled illustrations on topics such as parts of the body, clothes, position words, shapes and colours.
- **Grammar pages** provide help with understanding pronouns and question words.
- **Word banks** and **number banks** give help in learning and spelling time words, synonyms and antonyms, the seasons, measures, numbers and much-used words.

About *Collins First School Dictionary Skills*

Activity sheets

The activity sheets help you to use the *Collins First School Dictionary* as an active literacy resource. They provide a wide range of activities to help Y1 and Y2 (P2 and P3) children develop basic dictionary skills. They give you, the teacher, a variety of strategies to support literacy objectives.

The activity sheets are also suitable as a focus for class teaching, for use with a small group, or for individual work in class or at home. The range of activities enables you to select appropriate activity sheets to meet the needs of individual children.

The activity sheets are grouped in seven sections:

Using a dictionary
Activity sheets 1, 2 and 3 help children to understand the functions of a dictionary. Activity sheets 4 and 5 feature a sample page from the dictionary and explain how to read the information. It is advisable to introduce both of these activity sheets at the same time.

Alphabetical order
Activity sheets 6 to 11 support children in gaining alphabet skills, reinforce these skills and give practice in finding words in the dictionary.

Dictionary organization
Activity sheets 12 to 19 cover the alphabetic listing of headwords and other information provided in the dictionary, such as synonyms and antonyms, word collections and information in pictures and diagrams.

Definitions
Activity sheets 20 to 22 encourage the children to use the dictionary to find and check definitions, including multiple definitions of one word.

Spelling
Activity sheets 23 to 32 show how a dictionary can be used to check spelling. They cover rhyming words, vowel phonemes, compound words and plurals. Activity sheet 28 encourages the use of the Look, Say, Cover, Write, Check strategy.

Dictionary games and quizzes
Activity sheets 33 to 38 offer a variety of dictionary games and quizzes to consolidate the children's understanding of the various functions of a dictionary.

Word banks
Activity sheets 39 and 40 encourage the children to collect and classify in groups words of special interest. Activity sheet 40 may be used at any time that word banks are explored.

Teacher's notes

The teacher's notes help you by listing the learning objectives, advising on preparation and providing answers to the questions, activity sheet by activity sheet.

Where appropriate, suggestions are given for follow-up work.

The notes end with further ideas for using the *Collins First School Dictionary* in supporting literacy objectives.

Curriculum planning charts

Time-saving curriculum planning charts are provided for easy reference, to support you when planning your lesson. The National Literacy Strategy chart matches *Collins First School Dictionary Skills* to word, text and sentence level objectives for Y1 and Y2. The Scottish 5–14 Guidelines chart matches *Collins First School Dictionary Skills* to P1 and P2 attainment targets at levels A and B.

Collins First School Dictionary Skills and the National Literacy Strategy

Activity sheet	NLS objective
Using a dictionary	
1 **What is a dictionary? (1)** *understanding the functions of a dictionary*	**Year 1**, Term 2, Text level objective 20; **Year 2**, Term 2, Text level objective 16
2 **What is a dictionary? (2)** *understanding the functions of a dictionary*	**Year 1**, Term 2, Text level objective 20
3 **What is a dictionary? (3)** *understanding the functions of a dictionary*	**Year 1**, Term 2, Text level objective 20; **Year 2**, Term 2, Text level objective 17
4 **How to use a dictionary (1)** *understanding how information is presented*	**Year 1**, Term 2, Text level objective 20; **Year 2**, Term 2, Text level objective 16,17
5 **How to use a dictionary (2)** *understanding how information is presented*	**Year 1**, Term 2, Text level objective 20; **Year 2**, Term 2, Text level objective 16, 17
Alphabetical order	
6 **The alphabet** *filling in missing letters*	**Year 1**, Term 1, Word level objective 2
7 **Alphabetical order** *letters after, before and between*	**Year 1**, Term 1, Word level objective 2
8 **Alphabet fun** *putting letters into alphabetical order*	**Year 1**, Term 1, Word level objective 2
9 **Alphabetical order: the first letter (1)** *putting words into alphabetical order*	**Year 1**, Term 1, Word level objective 2
10 **Alphabetical order: the first letter (2)** *putting words into alphabetical order*	**Year 1**, Term 1, Word level objective 2
11 **Colour word search** *putting colours into alphabetical order*	**Year 1**, Term 1, Word level objective 2
Dictionary organization	
12 **A to Z** *understanding how words are sorted*	**Year 1**, Term 2, Text level objective 20; **Year 2**, Term 2, Text level objective 16
13 **Find the word (1)** *finding words, checking spelling*	**Year 1**, Term 2, Text level objective 20; **Year 2**, Term 2, Text level objective 16
14 **Find the word (2)** *finding words, checking spelling*	**Year 1**, Term 2, Text level objective 20; **Year 2**, Term 2, Text level objective 16
15 **Looking further (1)** *other information provided by a dictionary*	**Year 2**, Term 2, Text level objective 17
16 **Looking further (2)** *other information provided by a dictionary*	**Year 2**, Term 2, Text level objective 17
17 **Similar** *synonyms*	**Year 2**, Term 3, Word level objective 10
18 **Different** *antonyms*	**Year 2**, Term 2, Word level objective 11; **Year 3**, Term 2, Word level objective 24
19 **Find the word (3)** *finding the words, writing meanings*	**Year 1**, Term 2, Text level objective 20; **Year 2**, Term 2, Text level objective 16,17

Activity sheet	NLS objective
Definitions	
20 **Find the word (4)** *completing word in definition*	**Year 1**, Term 2, Text level objective 20; **Year 2**, Term 2, Text level objective 17
21 **Find the meaning** *matching word to definition*	**Year 1**, Term 2, Text level objective 20; **Year 2**, Term 2, Text level objective 17
22 **More than one meaning** *write the correct definition*	**Year 1**, Term 2, Text level objective 20; **Year 2**, Term 2, Text level objective 17; **Year 3**, Term 3, Word level objective 14
Spelling	
23 **Anagrams** *checking spelling*	**Year 1**, Term 2, Text level objective 20; **Year 3**, Term 2, Word level objective 19
24 **Rhyme time** *words with the same sound and spelling*	**Year 1**, Term 1, Word level objective 10
25 **The right spelling (1)** *long vowel phonemes; ai, ay, a-e; ee,ea; oa, o-e, ow*	**Year 1**, Term 3, Word level objective 1; **Year 2**, Term 1, Word level objective 1
26 **The right spelling (2)** *long vowel phonemes: ie, y, i-e, igh; oo, u-e, ew, ue*	**Year 1**, Term 3, Word level objective 1; **Year 2**, Term 1, Word level objective 3
27 **Building words** *compound words*	**Year 1**, Term 2, Word level objective 7; **Year 2**, Term 2, Word level objective 4
28 **More than one** *plurals*	**Year 1**, Term 2, Word level objective 8; **Year 3**, Term 2, Word level objective 11
29 **Verbs** *-s, -ed, and -ing endings*	**Year 1**, Term 2, Word level objective 6; **Year 2**, Term 1, Word level objective 7
30 **Sounds similar (1)** *ow and ou; oi and oy; short oo and u*	**Year 2**, Term 1, Word level objective 3
31 **Sounds similar (2)** *air, are, ere and ear*	**Year 2**, Term 1, Word level objective 2
32 **Look, Say, Cover, Write, Check** *how to learn spellings*	**Year 3**, Term1, Word level objective 7
Dictionary games and quizzes	
33 **Word fun** *crossword and alphabet code*	**Year 1**, Term 1, Word level objective 2; **Year 2**, Term 2, Text level objective 17
34 **Word search** *spelling*	**Year 3**, Term 2, Word level objective 19
35 **Musical instruments** *finding word, checking spelling*	**Year 1**, Term 2, Text level objective 20; **Year 3**, Term 2, Word level objective 19
36 **Word steps** *steps crossword*	**Year 1**, Term 1, Word level objective 2; **Year 2**, Term 2, Text level objective 17
37 **Quiz time (1)** *dictionary quiz*	**Year 1**, Term 1, Text level objective 20; **Year 2**, Term 2, Text level objective 17
38 **Quiz time (2)** *dictionary quiz*	**Year 1**, Term 1, Text level objective 20; **Year 2**, Term 2, Text level objective 17
Word banks	
39 **Making a word bank** *how to make a word bank*	**Year 1**, Term 2, Text level objective 20, Word level objective 10; **Year 2**, Term 2, Text level objective 17
40 **Collecting words** *template for children's personal word bank*	**Year 1**, Term 2, Word level objective 10; **Year 1**, Term 3, Word level objective 8; **Year 2**, Term 2, Word level objective 10; **Year 2**, Term 3, Word level objective 9

Collins First School Dictionary Skills and the Scottish 5–14 Guidelines

P2/3 attainment targets at Level A/B

Activity sheet number

	1	2	3	4	5	6	7	8	9	10	11	12	13	14	15	16	17	18	19	20	21	22	23	24	25	26	27	28	29	30	31	32	33	34	35	36	37	38	39	40
Reading for information																																								
*awareness of letter sequence	✓	✓	✓			✓	✓	✓																																
*first letter order	✓	✓	✓	✓	✓	✓	✓	✓	✓	✓	✓	✓	✓	✓					✓														✓				✓			
*locating specific information															✓	✓			✓	✓	✓	✓							✓				✓			✓	✓	✓	✓	
Awareness of genre																																								
*recognizing page layouts			✓	✓	✓					✓		✓	✓	✓																										
Functional writing																				✓		✓			✓	✓														
Spelling																																								
*look, cover, write, check	✓	✓	✓								✓						✓	✓					✓	✓	✓	✓	✓	✓	✓	✓	✓	✓		✓	✓	✓				✓
*rhyming families																								✓						✓	✓									
*spelling rules																									✓	✓		✓	✓	✓	✓									
Knowledge about language				✓	✓				✓	✓			✓	✓			✓	✓	✓			✓						✓	✓											

Collins First School Dictionary Skills Activity Sheets

Using a dictionary

Alphabetical order

Dictionary organization

Definitions

Spelling

Dictionary games and quizzes

Word banks

Teacher's notes

Using a dictionary

Activity 1 What is a dictionary? (1)

Learning objective: *to understand the functions of a dictionary*

Before you start

- Ask the children to explain what they think a dictionary is used for. Encourage them to understand its usefulness in finding spellings and definitions.
- Ask them to investigate how words are listed in a dictionary, that is, alphabetically. Give practice in finding the first and last words which begin with certain letters, such as *h*, *m*, *q*, *e*, *x*, *g*.
- Select words from the dictionary and encourage the children to find them as quickly as they can. Ask them to read aloud the definitions.
- Invite the children to find the correct spellings of selected words.

Answers Alphabetical order: a; baby, jacket, table, zebra

Activity 2 What is a dictionary? (2)

Learning objective: *to understand the functions of a dictionary*

Before you start

- Ask the children to explain again what they think a dictionary is used for. Remind them of its usefulness in finding spellings and definitions.
- Ask them to investigate how words are listed in a dictionary, that is, alphabetically. Give practice in finding the first and last words which begin with certain letters, such as *c*, *f*, *j*, *u*, *t*, *s*.
- Select words from the dictionary and encourage the children to find them as quickly as they can. Ask them to read aloud the definitions.
- Invite the children to find the correct spellings of selected words.

Answers Spelling: almost, cupboard, muddy, climb

Activity 3

What is a dictionary? (3)

***Learning objective:** to understand the functions of a dictionary*

Before you start

- Ask the children to describe the uses of a dictionary.
- Ask them to explain how words are listed in a dictionary. Give further practice in finding the first and last words which begin with certain letters, such as *b*, *i*, *n*, *d*, *v*, *k*.
- Select words from the dictionary and encourage the children to find them as quickly as they can. Ask them to read aloud the definitions.
- Invite the children to find the correct spellings of selected words.

Answers

A **lorry** is a large vehicle. It carries big things by road.
A **valley** is a low area of land between hills or mountains.
A **log** is a large piece of wood from a tree.

Activity 4

How to use a dictionary (1)

***Learning objective:** to understand how information is presented in a dictionary*

Before you start

This page is a useful reference sheet for individual use or display.

- Ask the children to open their copies of *Collins First School Dictionary* at page 42. Discuss the way the page is set out, drawing attention to guide words, the alphabet line and headwords. Emphasize that the vertical alphabet line acts as a reminder of alphabetical order.

  Point out how different sorts of type are used for these different parts.
- Taking each aspect in turn, explain how each can be used to help the children find and use the information they require.
- Select different pages and ask the children to identify the various elements previously discussed.

Activity 5 How to use a dictionary (2)

Learning objective: *to understand how information is presented in a dictionary*

Before you start

This page is a useful reference sheet for individual use or display.

- Ask the children to again open their copies of *Collins First School Dictionary* at page 42. Point out the way the page is set out, drawing attention to definitions, the other forms of the headwords (for example, *deeper*, *deepest*) and the use of examples to show how a word is used. Remind them that the vertical alphabet line helps them to remember alphabetical order.

  Again stress how different sorts of type are used for these different parts.
- Explain each aspect in turn, saying how each can be used to help the children find and use the information they require.
- Select different pages and ask the children to identify the various elements previously discussed.

Alphabetical order

Activity 6 The alphabet

Learning objective: *to practise and secure alphabetic knowledge and alphabetical order*

Before you start

- Revise the names and sounds of the letters of the alphabet. Demonstrate them in lower and upper case.
- Ask the children to recite the alphabet in unison.
- Ask someone to begin reciting the alphabet. Then point to a second child to continue for a few letters, and so on.

Answers

ab**c**d**e**f g**h**ijk**l** mno**p**qr**s** tu**v**w**x**y**z**

Activity 7

Alphabetical order

Learning objective: *to practise and secure knowledge of alphabetical order*

Before you start

- Revise the complete alphabet.
- Invite the children to name the letters which come *before* selected letters in the alphabet.
- Do the same with letters which come *after* selected letters.

Answers

1. efg**h** lmn**o** **q**rst **u**vwx b**c**de hi**j**k m**n**op 2. l, x, u, i, q, f, d, j, s, v
3. b, l, i, x, f, u, e, w, n, s 4. c, o, g, w, l, y, t, q, i, u

---

Activity 8

Alphabet fun

Learning objective: *to practise and secure knowledge of alphabetical order*

Before you start

- Revise alphabetical order.
- Offer the children three or four letters at random and invite them to put the letters in alphabetical order.

Answers

1. bcde ghij mnopq vwxyz 2. bcfg qstv hikm ptvw
3.

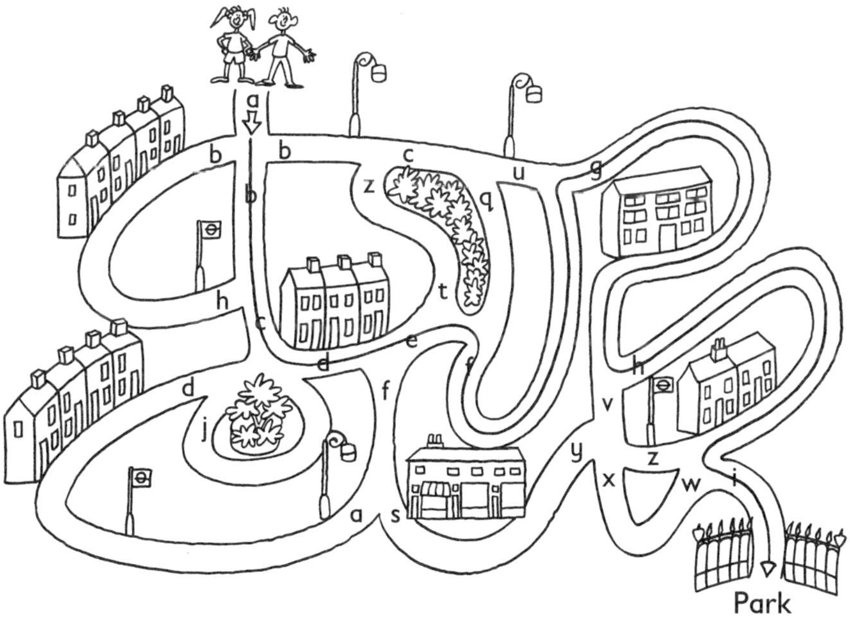

Activity 9 Alphabetical order: the first letter (1)

☐ ***Learning objective:*** *to organize words alphabetically using the first letter*

Before you start

- Ensure the children can identify the initial letter in selected words.
- Show how we can use initial letters to sort words into alphabetical order.
- Practise this with a number of selected words or those suggested by the children.

Answers

1. alligator, bear, camel, dog
2. apple, lemon, orange, peach; hat, jeans, scarf, tie

More to do

- Show how the children's own names can be sorted into alphabetical order.

Activity 10 Alphabetical order: the first letter (2)

☐ ***Learning objective:*** *to organize words alphabetically using the first letter*

Before you start

- Revise how we can use initial letters to sort words into alphabetical order.
- Make short lists of the children's favourite foods, sports, activities, toys or other things. Ensure that no two words begin with the same letter. Revise how to sort these words into alphabetical order.

Answers

drum, piano, xylophone
carrot, egg, toast
doctor, nurse, teacher
car, truck, van
factory, hospital, school

More to do

- Ask the children to find some of the above words in the dictionary. What definitions does the dictionary give for them?

Activity 11 Colour word search

☐ ***Learning objective:*** *to organize words alphabetically using the first letter*

Before you start

- Ask the children what their favourite colours are. Make a list, ensuring that no two colours begin with the same letter. Encourage the children to sort them into alphabetical order.
- Ring one colour in the word search to show them how to do it. You could use an enlarged copy of the activity sheet.

Answers

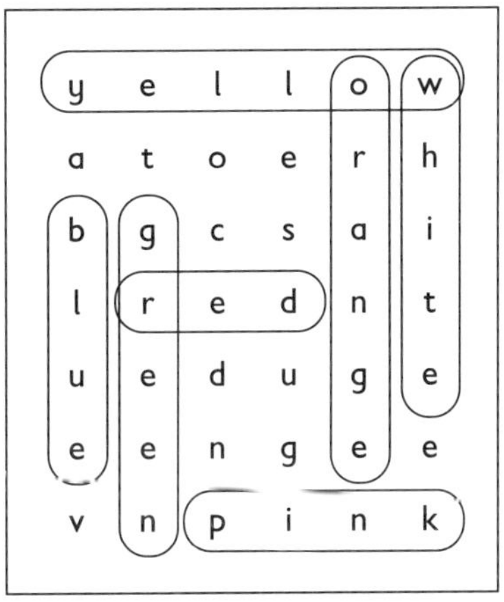

(in alphabetical order): blue, green, orange, pink, red, white, yellow

More to do

- Encourage the children to use activity sheet 40 to make a word bank of colour words.

  Ask them to use a crayon to match each colour to its name.
- Use activity sheet 32 to encourage the children to use the Look, Say, Cover, Write, Check strategy for learning the spellings of the more common colours.

Dictionary organization

Activity 12 A to Z

Learning objective: *to use simple dictionaries and to understand their alphabetical organization*

Before you start

- Revise alphabetical order.
- Ask the children to find the first word in the dictionary beginning with selected letters.
- Do the same with the last word for selected letters.
- Remind the children how the alphabet line in the dictionary can be used to remind them of alphabetical order.

Answers

1. abacus
2. zoo
3. baby, kangaroo, machine, pack, vacuum cleaner, zebra
4. cylinder, dying, just, own, rush, wrote

Activity 13 Find the word (1)

Learning objective: *to use simple dictionaries and to understand their alphabetical organization*

Before you start

- Ask the children to identify the words pictured on the activity sheet and the initial letter of those words.
- Challenge them to find the words in the dictionary, noting the page number.

Answers

bicycle, page 18; lighthouse, page 86; skateboard, page 136;
wasp, page 164; tiger, page 154; mountain, page 95;
seesaw, page 130; rope, page 125; windmill, page 167

Activity 14 Find the word (2)

Learning objective: *to use simple dictionaries and to understand their alphabetical organization*

Before you start

- Ask the children to identify the words pictured on the activity sheet and the initial letter of those words.
- Invite them to find the words in the dictionary, making a note of the page numbers.

Answers

ladybird, page 82; trumpet, page 158; parrot, page 105
squirrel, page 143; arrow, page 12; key, page 80
umbrella, page 160; dice, page 43; hammer, page 68
jug, page 79; pencil, page 107; whistle, page 166

Activity 15 Looking further (1)

Learning objective: *to explore other information provided in a dictionary*

Before you start

- Introduce the children to the information at the back of the *Collins First School Dictionary* (pages 172–184). Explore the variety of information given there.
- Focus on one section: **Dinosaurs**. Ask the children questions such as: *What did Triceratops use its three horns for?* or *Which flying creature lived at the same time as the dinosaurs?*
- Ask the children several questions to which the answers may be found on those pages: *How many sides has a star shape?* Encourage the children to locate the correct section and then the relevant information within that section.

Answers

1. Wednesday **2.** July **3.** afternoon
4. how, what, when, where, who, why, which **5.** 1 000 000
6. six **7.** eye, eyebrow, forehead or eyelashes

Activity 16 Looking further (2)

Learning objective: *to explore other information provided in a dictionary*

Before you start

- Revisit the information at the back of the *Collins First School Dictionary* (pages 172–184). Explore the variety of information given there.
- Focus on one section: **Dinosaurs**. Ask the children questions such as: *What did a brontosaurus eat? Why did the stegosaurus have bony plates?*
- Ask the children several questions to which the answers may be found on those pages: *How many sides has a pentagon?* Encourage the children to locate the correct section and then the relevant information within that section.

Answers

1. false 2. true 3. true 4. false 5. true 6. true
7. octagon, pentagon, kite, hexagon

Activity 17 Similar

Learning objective: *to explore synonyms*

Before you start

- Focus on the **Synonyms** section at the back of the dictionary (page 180).
- Give practice in finding suitable synonyms for selected words.

Answers

1. small, neat, sad
2. scared, quick, shout, bake

More to do

- Encourage the children to make their own word banks of synonyms, using activity sheet 40.

Activity 18

Different

Learning objective: *to explore antonyms*

Before you start

- Focus on the **Antonyms** section at the back of the dictionary (page 181).
- Give practice in finding suitable antonyms for selected words.

Answers

1. hard, light, wide, noisy, many, inside
2. high, low; heavy, light; back, front

More to do

- Encourage the children to make their own word banks of antonyms, using activity sheet 40.

Activity 19

Find the word (3)

Learning objective: *to explore simple definitions in dictionaries*

Before you start

- Revise alphabetical order.
- Practise finding selected words in the dictionary as quickly as possible. Ask the children to say which words come *before* and *after* each given word.
- Invite the children to locate and tell you the meanings of selected words.

Answers

1. alien, wall, stare, fantastic, cliff, train
2. few: not many; stream: a small river; poet: a person who writes poems; kettle: people boil water in a kettle; zoo: animals are kept in a zoo so that people can look at them

More to do

- Ask the children to give their own definitions of words you select, and then to check the dictionary definition. Discuss any differences between the two.

Definitions

Activity 20 Find the word (4)

Learning objective: *to locate words by the initial letter and check the definition*

Before you start

- Ask the children to suggest answers to questions such as: *Which word beginning with **i** means a piece of land that has water all around it?* Then ask the children to check their answers in the dictionary.

Answers

1. rug **2.** calf **3.** ocean **4.** woman **5.** salt/sugar **6.** medicine **7.** desk **8.** peanut **9.** water **10.** kitchen

More to do

- Encourage the children to use the dictionary to make up their own questions similar to those on activity sheets 15 and 16.

Activity 21 Find the meaning

Learning objective: *to explore simple definitions in dictionaries*

Before you start

- Invite the children to find the definitions of selected words.
- Give the definitions of selected words in the dictionary. Discuss what words might fit the definitions. Ask the children to look up the words they think are defined to check their ideas.

Answers

1. diamond: a hard bright jewel; pirate: a sailor who attacks and robs other ships; spaceship: a vehicle that can travel through space; wolf: a wild animal like a large dog; insect: a tiny animal with six legs
2. school: children go here to learn; pen: you use this when you write or draw with ink; monster: a huge, frightening creature; desert: a hot, dry place

Activity 22 More than one meaning

Learning objective: *to explore words with more than one meaning*

Before you start

- Find selected words in the dictionary which have two or more definitions, such as *play*. Invent a sentence with the word in it: *We went to see a play last night.* Ask the children to tell you which of the dictionary definitions describes the use of that word.
- Discuss which part of speech the word is in a particular sentence: noun or verb. Ask the children to justify their answers.

Answers

1. A match is a little stick that people use to light a fire.
2. Squash is a drink made from fruit, sugar and water.
3. a large open space with grass and trees. People walk and play in parks.
4. If you trip over something, you catch your foot on it and fall over.
5. A stick is a long, thin piece of wood.

More to do

- Ask the children to find words in the dictionary with more than one meaning. Then ask them to make up their own sentences showing the different meanings.

Spelling

Activity 23 Anagrams

Learning objective: *to explore the spelling of familiar words*

Before you start

- Explain what an anagram is. Give examples of anagrams of short common words, using things that can be seen in the classroom: *xob (box), kobo (book), nep (pen).*

Answers

ape (11), wolf (168), badger (14), leaf (84), rose (125), loaf (87), pear (107), peach (107), face (54)

Activity 24 Rhyme time

☐ ***Learning objective:*** *to investigate rhyming patterns in words*

Before you start

- Invite the children to suggest rhyming words with common patterns, such as *bin*, *lake*, *moon*. Build up rhyming word banks.

Answers

hen; ring; clock; shop; train; cold; chair; park

More to do

- Ask the children to find definitions for the words in the rhyming word banks you made earlier. Alternatively, ask them to write their own definitions for those words and then compare the dictionary definitions.

Activity 25 The right spelling (1)

☐ ***Learning objective:*** *to explore the spelling of the long vowel phonemes* ***a, e*** *and* ***o***

Before you start

- Explore words with long vowel phonemes: ai, ay, a-e; ee, ea; oa, ow, o-e.
- Ask the children to put the words discussed in sentences to show their meaning.

Answers

Long **a**: gate, play, train; long **e**: leaf, tree, feet; long **o**: pole, boat, bow

---

Activity 26 The right spelling (2)

☐ ***Learning objective:*** *to explore the spelling of the long vowel phonemes* ***i*** *and* ***u***

Before you start

- Explore words with long vowel phonemes: ie, i-e, igh, y; oo, u-e, ew, ue
- Ask the children to put the words in sentences to show their meaning.

Answers

Long **i**: cry, bite, lie; It goes **high** in the sky.
Long **u**: moon, tune, flew; Use **glue** to stick things together.

More to do

- Encourage the children to make their own word banks of words with long vowel phonemes, using activity sheet 40.

Activity 27 Building words

Learning objective: *to explore compound words*

Before you start

- Ask the children to identify the separate words in compound words, for example, *cup* and *board* in cupboard.
- Practise building compound words.

Answers

1. lighthouse, football
2. classroom, blackboard, doorbell, motorbike, playground, toothbrush, thunderstorm, newspaper, butterfly

Activity 28 More than one

Learning objective: *to explore plurals, using the dictionary as reference*

Before you start

- Explore the most common ways of making plurals: by adding *s* and *es*.
- Show the children how the dictionary may be used to check the plurals of nouns.
- Give the children a list of selected nouns. Ask them to find the plurals in the dictionary.

Answers

1. ducks, mountains, bushes, shelves, babies, potatoes
2. houses, strawberries, leaves, branches

More to do

- Discuss irregular plurals such as *mice*, *teeth*, *children* and so on.

Activity 29 Verbs

Learning objective: *to explore verb tense by adding -s, -ing and -ed, using the dictionary as reference*

Before you start

- Explore verb tense made by adding -s, -ing and -ed.
- Identify common verbs which do not make their past tense by adding -ed: *ran*, *swam*, *read*, *wrote*.
- Show how the dictionary may be used to check the different forms and tenses of verbs.

Answers

1. smiles, smiling, smiled
2. buries, burying, buried
3. walks, walking, walked
4. carries, carrying, carried
5. laughs, laughing, laughed
6. cries, crying, cried
7. hurries, hurrying, hurried
8. dives, diving, dived
9. slips, slipping, slipped
10. barks, barking, barked

Activity 30 Sounds similar (1)

Learning objective: *to investigate the common spelling patterns for the vowel phonemes* ***ow, oy*** *and* ***oo***

Before you start

- Explore how the same sound can be spelled differently in words such as h**ow** and l**ou**d; b**oy** and c**oi**n; p**u**sh and b**oo**k.

Answers

ow and ou: cloud, crowd, shout

oi and oy: boil, toy, coin

oo and u: book, push/pushchair, foot

More to do

- Encourage the children to make a word bank of words in which the same sound is spelled differently.

Activity 31 Sounds similar (2)

☐ ***Learning objective:*** *to investigate the common spelling patterns for the vowel phoneme* ***air***

Before you start

- Explore the the common spelling patterns for the phoneme **air**: st**air**s, b**ear**, m**are**, th**ere**.
- Ask the children to use the words in sentences to show their meanings.

Answers

fair, pear, share; Did you t**ear** this dress? It is rude to st**are**.
Her h**air** was very long. Take c**are**. The st**air**s are steep.
Wh**ere** will you w**ear** that hat?

Activity 32 Look, Say, Cover, Write, Check

☐ ***Learning objective:*** *to encourage the use of the Look, Say, Cover, Write, Check strategy for learning spellings*

Before you start

- Show the children how to use the Look, Say, Cover, Write, Check strategy for learning spellings.
- Encourage them to use the activity sheet guide to learn difficult spellings.

Dictionary games and quizzes

Activity 33 Word fun

Learning objectives: *to locate words from initial letters and check definitions; to practise putting words into alphabetical order*

Before you start

- Show the children how to use a dictionary to help them with crossword clues.
- Revise alphabetical order.

Answers

	1 c	a	r	a	v	a	n	
			2 e	l	b	o	w	
		3 r	u	l	e	r		
		4 t	w	i	c	e		
		5 y	o	g	u	r	t	
6 F	r	i	d	a	y			
	7 m	i	s	t	a	k	e	
			8 w	o	b	b	l	y
		9 s	t	r	o	n	g	

The animal's name contained in the puzzle is **alligator**.

Coded message: Bring drinks for our picnic tomorrow Zoe

Activity 34 Word search

☐ ***Learning objective:*** *to identify the names of familiar animals and spell them correctly*

Before you start

- Let the children practise finding one or two animal names in the word search.

Answers

a	c	o	t	t	e	r	t
l	h	a	m	s	t	e	r
t	i	g	e	p	p	i	g
n	m	y	r	j	f	w	r
p	p	i	n	c	d	s	l
r	a	b	b	i	t	y	h
f	n	l	g	u	m	v	o
o	z	x	d	a	a	d	r
x	e	y	c	a	e	r	s
z	e	b	r	a	m	s	e

Activity 35 Musical instruments

☐ ***Learning objective:*** *to identify the names of common musical instruments and check their spellings*

Before you start

- Ask the children to identify the musical instruments on the activity sheet.

Answers

1. drum, violin, recorder, piano, trumpet, xylophone, guitar
2. orchestra

Activity 36 Word steps

Learning objective: *to use a dictionary to solve a crossword, locating words by use of the first letter and checking the definitions*

Before you start

- Ask the children to find the first three words in the word steps. Encourage them to use the dictionary to help them, especially with the correct spellings.

Answers

ache, echo, oval, lean, news, sigh, hero, obey, your, roar, rare

More to do

- Encourage the children to make up their own word steps with clues.

Activity 37 Quiz time (1)

Learning objective: *to use a dictionary to find a word from its definition*

Before you start

- Revise how to find a word from its initial letter and definition.

Answers

army, boat, chick, dustbin, emerald, February,
gate, honey, iron, jug, kite, lamb, marmalade

Activity 38 Quiz time (2)

Learning objective: *to use a dictionary to find a word from its definition*

Before you start

- This activity sheet is a continuation of the quiz on activity sheet 37.

Answers

night, onion, pebble, quack, rubbish, seat, toad, uncle, vet, winner, X-ray, yolk, zigzag

More to do

- Encourage the children to make up their own dictionary quiz.

Word banks

Activity 39 Making a word bank

Learning objective: *to encourage the children to collect and classify words*

Before you start

- Discuss how to classify the words on the activity sheet.
- Encourage the children to use the information at the back of the dictionary to find more words to add to their word bank.

Answers

Clothes: trousers, tie, blouse, trainers
Time words: March, Sunday, year, afternoon, morning
Parts of the body: wrist, knee, elbow
Parts of a car: windscreen, bumper, headlight, engine

Activity 40 Collecting words

Learning objective: *to encourage children to build individual collections of personal interest or significant words*

Before you start

- This activity sheet may be used at any time for the children to make their own word banks.
- Encourage the children to find out the meanings and to learn the spellings of words in their collections.

Further ideas to support literacy objectives

Word level work

- Use the dictionary to investigate, read and spell words ending in *ff*, *ll*, *ss*, *ck*, *ng*. Ask the children to search out words with these endings and make word banks.
- Make collections of words with the initial consonant clusters *bl*, *cr*, *tr* and *str*. Use the Look, Say, Cover, Write, Check strategy to learn how to spell them.

- Use the dictionary to investigate the spelling of words with final consonant clusters such as *nd*, *lp* and *st*.
- Look up *vowel* and *consonant* in the dictionary to find out the difference. Identify vowels and consonants in selected words.
- Explore the use of *a* and *an*. Ask the children to work out the rule for their use.
- Collect and investigate the spelling of words with the vowel digraphs *wh*, *ph*, *ch* (as in *character*).
- Investigate words with *-ful* and *-ly* endings.
- Ask the children to select words from the dictionary for their own spelling quiz. The children who ask the questions should be able to spell their own words! Encourage them to check the answers in the dictionary.
- Give each child 26 slips of paper and ask them to write one word on each slip for every letter of the alphabet, using the dictionary. Ask them to mix up the slips and then rearrange them in alphabetical order.
- Using the same slips of paper, invite the children to spell the words or give you a definition. Check their answers in the dictionary.
- Choose a word from the dictionary with more than one meaning. Ask the children to give their own definition for each meaning. Check in the dictionary. Discuss any differences.

Sentence level work

- Use the dictionary to check the past tense of irregular verbs.
- Collect and classify examples of similar verbs, such as *speak*, *shout*, *whisper*. Discuss the shades of meaning and ask the children to write sentences to show these differences.
- Encourage the children to make their own dictionary quiz. Questions may be grouped by letters of the alphabet. For example, the answers to a particular group of questions might all begin with the letter *t*.

Text level work

- Encourage the children to use their phonological, contextual, grammatical and graphic knowledge to work out and predict the meanings of unfamiliar words in their reading, and then to use the dictionary to check the meaning.
- Use the material at the back of the *Collins First School Dictionary* to locate parts of text that give particular information such as labelled diagrams: parts of the body, parts of a bicycle and car, items of clothing, position words. Encourage the children to make their own labelled diagrams of familiar things such as a computer or a building.
- Make class dictionaries and glossaries of special interest words. Use the *Collins First School Dictionary* as a model. Include other forms of words and examples of how a word is used. Include illustrations where appropriate.

Activity 1 Name ______________________________

What is a dictionary? (1)

A dictionary is a book that lists words in alphabetical order. It tells you how to spell them and what they mean.

Alphabetical order

What letter does the word **abacus** begin with? ________

Look in the *Collins First School Dictionary*.

What is the first word beginning with **b** in the dictionary? ______________________

What is the first word beginning with **j**? ______________________

What is the first word beginning with **t**? ______________________

What is the first word beginning with **z**? ______________________

Activity 2 Name ______________________________

What is a dictionary? (2)

A dictionary is a book that lists words in alphabetical order. It tells you how to spell them and what they mean.

Spelling

If you are not sure how to spell a word, a dictionary is the place to find out.
Use your dictionary to find which is the correct spelling of the words below.

almost or **allmost**? ____________________

cuboard or **cupboard**? ____________________

mudy or **muddy**? ____________________

climb or **clime**? ____________________

Activity 3 Name

What is a dictionary? (3)

A dictionary is a book that lists words in alphabetical order. It tells you how to spell them and what they mean.

What words mean

A dictionary tells you what each word means. This is what the dictionary tells you about the word **jug**:

> **jug** jugs
> A **jug** is a container for holding liquids.
> It has a handle and a lip for pouring.

Find each of these words in your dictionary and write its meaning.

lorry

valley

log

Name ______________________________

How to use a dictionary (1)

The words in the dictionary are listed in a special way to help you find the information you need.

Guide words

Guide words are printed in very large letters at the top of each page. The guide word on the left page tells you the first word on that page. The guide word on the right page tells you the last word on that page.

Alphabet line

The alphabet line makes the dictionary easy to use by reminding you of alphabetical order. The letter in the coloured box is the first letter of each word on that page.

Headwords

Headwords are the words you look up in the dictionary. They are listed in alphabetical order and printed in blue letters.

December

a b c **Dd** e f g h i j k l m n o p q r s t u v w x y z

December
December is the twelfth month of the year. It has 31 days.

decide **decides, deciding, decided**
You **decide** when you choose between two or more things.

deck **decks**
A **deck** is one of the floors of a ship or bus.
*Tom sat on the top **deck** of the bus.*

decorate **decorates, decorating, decorated**
1 If you **decorate** something, you make it look nice.
*Mum and I **decorated** the cake with icing.*
2 If you **decorate** a room, you paint it or paper the walls.

deep **deeper, deepest**
When something is **deep**, it is a long way down to its bottom.
*Be careful! The water is very **deep** here.*

deer **deer**
A **deer** is a large wild animal.
The male **deer** may have horns called antlers.

42

Activity 5

Name ______________________________

How to use a dictionary (2)

The words in the dictionary are listed in a special way to help you find the information you need.

Definitions

The definition of a word is what it means. Definitions are printed in ordinary type. When a word has more than one meaning, the different meanings are numbered.

Other forms of a word

Next to each headword are other forms of the same word. These are printed in smaller letters than the headword.

Example sentences

Sometimes the dictionary gives you a sentence as an example to help you understand how a word is used.

a b c **Dd** e f g h i j k l m n o p q r s t u v w x y z

December
December is the twelfth month of the year. It has 31 days.

decide **decides, deciding, decided**
You **decide** when you choose between two or more things.

deck **decks**
A **deck** is one of the floors of a ship or bus.
*Tom sat on the top **deck** of the bus.*

decorate **decorates, decorating, decorated**
1 If you **decorate** something, you make it look nice.
*Mum and I **decorated** the cake with icing.*
2 If you **decorate** a room, you paint it or paper the walls.

deep **deeper, deepest**
When something is **deep**, it is a long way down to its bottom.
*Be careful! The water is very **deep** here.*

deer **deer**
A **deer** is a large wild animal.
The male **deer** may have horns called antlers.

Activity 6 Name ______________________________

The alphabet

Fill in the missing letters of the alphabet.

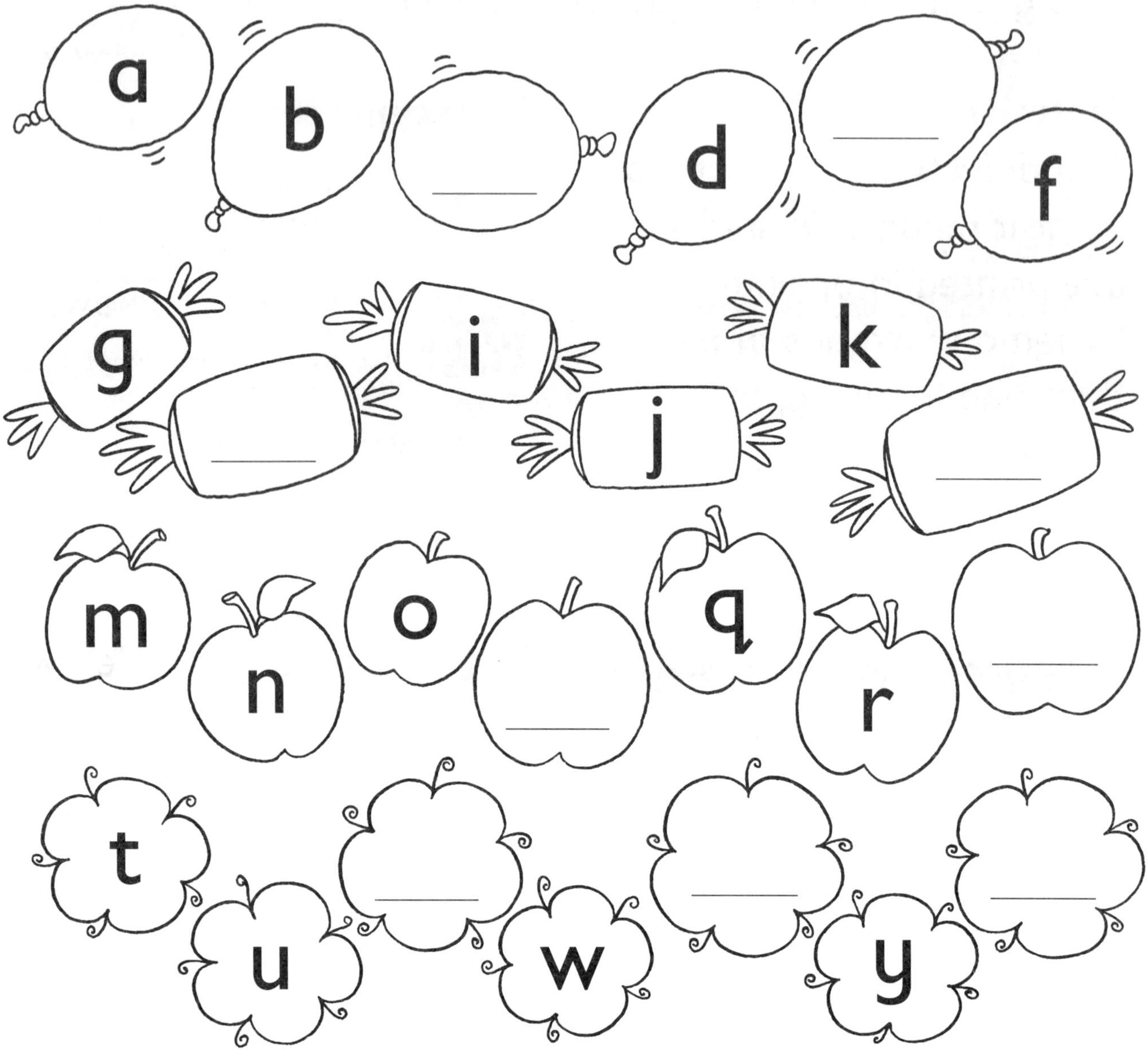

Write the alphabet here.

____

____

a b c d e f g h i j k l m n o p q r s t u v w x y z

Activity 7 Name ______________________________

Alphabetical order

1. Write each missing letter.

e f g ___ l m n ___ ___ r s t ___ v w x

b ___ d e h i ___ k m ___ o p

2. Write the letter which comes **after** each letter below:

k ___ w ___ t ___ h ___ p ___

e ___ c ___ i ___ r ___ u ___

3. Write the letter which comes **before** each letter below:

___ c ___ m ___ j ___ y ___ g

___ v ___ f ___ x ___ o ___ t

4. Write the letter which comes **between** the two letters below:

b and d ___ n and p ___ f and h ___ v and x ___

k and m ___ x and z ___ s and u ___ p and r ___

h and j ___ t and v ___

a	b	c	d	e	f	g	h	i	j	k	l	m	n	o	p	q	r	s	t	u	v	w	x	y	z

Activity 8 Name ______________________________

Alphabet fun

1. Put these groups of letters into alphabetical order.

c b e d　　i h g j　　p n q m o　　w z x v y

______　______　______　______

2. Do the same with these.

f c b g　　t s v q　　k h m i　　v t p w

______　______　______　______

3. Which way do Li and Sam go to get to the park?
Follow the letters in alphabetical order to find out.

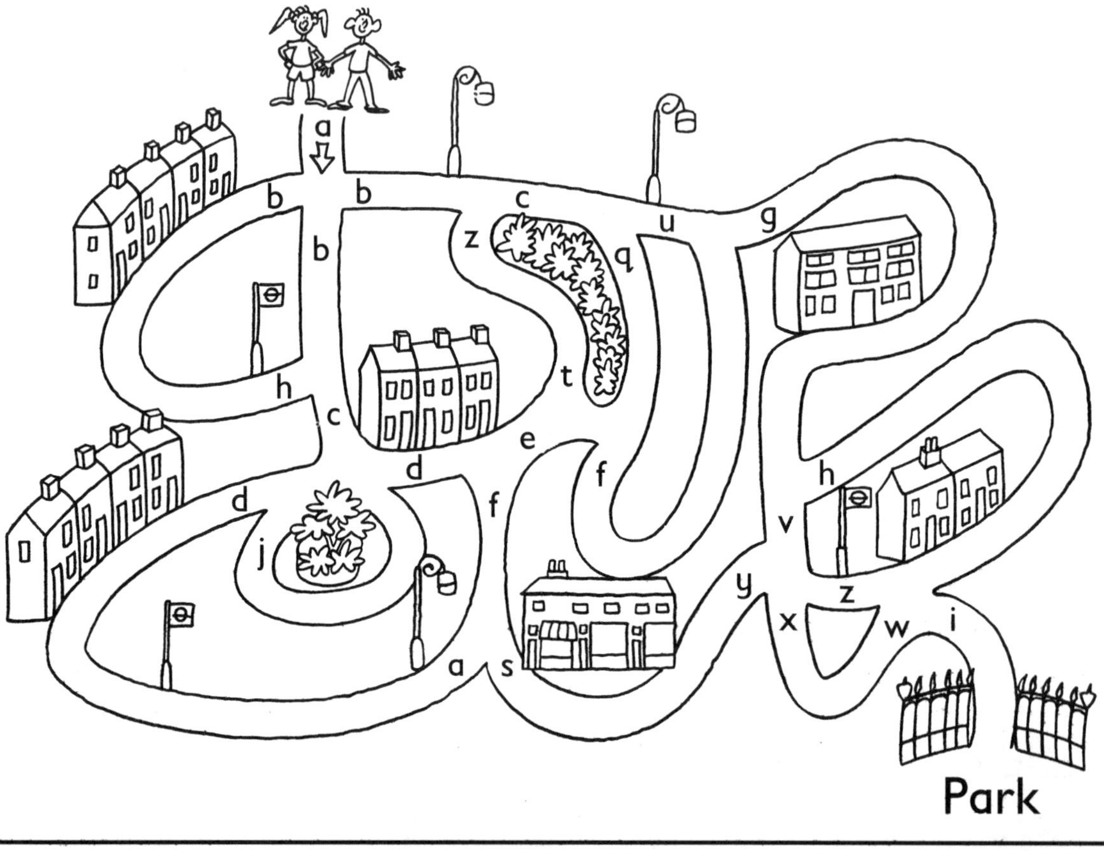

a b c d e f g h i j k l m n o p q r s t u v w x y z

Activity 9 Name ______________________

Alphabetical order: the first letter (1)

1. Put a ring round the first letter of each of these words.

dog

camel

bear

alligator

Now put the words in alphabetical order. The first one has been done for you.

alligator ______________ ______________ ______________

2. Do the same for these words, line by line.

lemon

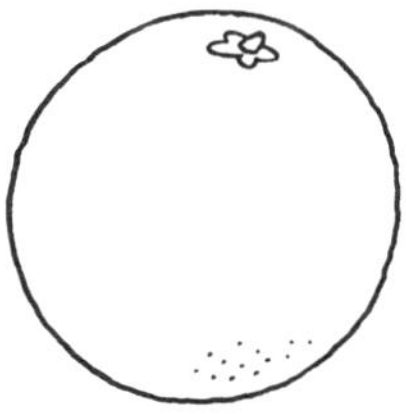
orange

apple

peach

______________ ______________ ______________ ______________

scarf

jeans

hat

tie

______________ ______________ ______________ ______________

a b c d e f g h i j k l m n o p q r s t u v w x y z

Activity 10 Name ______________________

Alphabetical order: the first letter (2)

Write each row of words in alphabetical order.

piano	xylophone	drum
______	______	______

toast	carrot	egg
______	______	______
doctor	teacher	nurse
______	______	______

truck	car	van
______	______	______
hospital	school	factory
______	______	______

a b c d e f g h i j k l m n o p q r s t u v w x y z

Activity 11 Name ____________________

Colour word search

There are seven colour words hidden in this soap bubble. Can you find them?

y	e	l	l	o	w
a	t	o	e	r	h
b	g	c	s	a	i
l	r	e	d	n	t
u	e	d	u	g	e
e	e	n	g	e	e
v	n	p	i	n	k

Write the colours you found.

__________ __________ __________

__________ __________ __________ __________

Now put the colours you found into alphabetical order.

__________ __________ __________

__________ __________ __________ __________

a b c d e f g h i j k l m n o p q r s t u v w x y z

Activity 12

Name ____________________

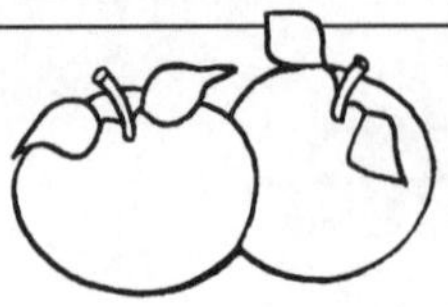

A to Z

The words in a dictionary are sorted into alphabetical order. Words starting with **a** come first, then those starting with **b**, then **c** and so on.

1. What is the first word in the *Collins First School Dictionary*? ____________

2. What is the last word in the dictionary? ____________

3. Find the **first** word which starts with the letters below.

   ? ? | b k m p v z | ? ?

   ____________ ____________ ____________

   ____________ ____________ ____________

4. Find the **last** word which starts with the letters below.

   ? ? | c d j o r w | ? ?

   ____________ ____________ ____________

   ____________ ____________ ____________

a b c d e f g h i j k l m n o p q r s t u v w x y z

Activity 13 Name ______________________________

Find the word (1)

Write the correct word for each picture. Check the spelling in your dictionary and write the page number you found it on.

____

page ______

____

page ______

____

page ______

____

page ______

____

page ______

____

page ______

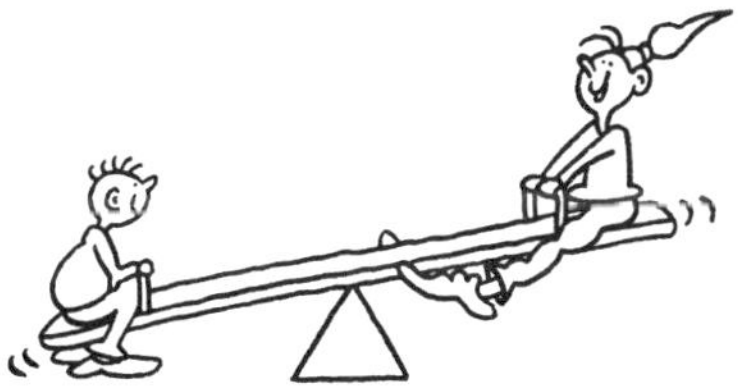

____

page ______

____

page ______

____

page ______

Activity 14 Name ______________________________

Find the word (2)

Write the correct word for each picture. Check the spelling in your dictionary and write the page number you found it on.

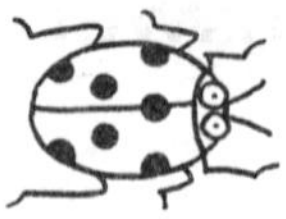

____

page ______

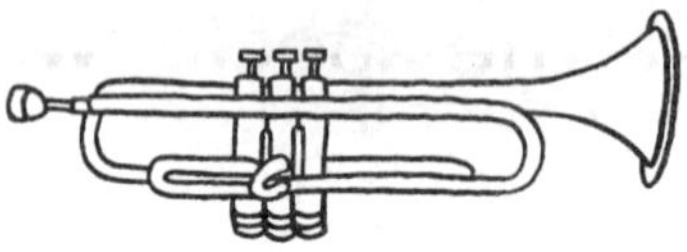

____

page ______

____

page ______

____

page ______

____

page ______

____

page ______

____

page ______

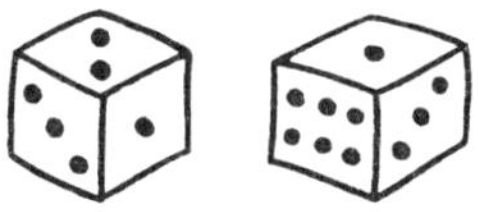

____

page ______

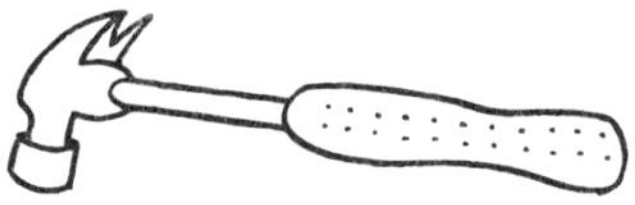

____

page ______

____

page ______

____

page ______

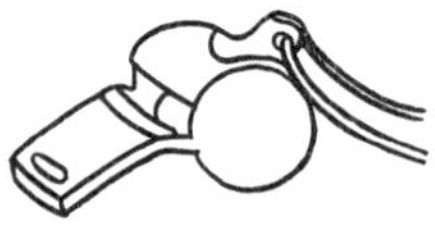

____

page ______

Activity 15 Name ____________________

Looking further (1)

Look at the back of the *Collins First School Dictionary*. There you will find lists of special words about dinosaurs, parts of the body, words to do with time, numbers and other information. Use the special words to answer the following questions.

1. Which day comes before **Thursday**? ______________

2. What is the 7th **month of the year**? ______________

3. Which comes first, **afternoon**

   or **evening**? ______________

4. Write seven **words we use to ask questions**.

   ____

5. Write **one million** in figures. ______________

6. How many sides does a **hexagon** have? ______________

7. Write the names of three parts of the **face** which are above the nose.

   a) ______________ b) ______________

   c) ______________

Activity 16 Name ______________________________

Looking further (2)

Look at the back of the *Collins First School Dictionary*. There you will find lists of special words about dinosaurs, parts of the body, words to do with time, numbers and other information. Use the special words to answer the following questions.

Answer **true** or **false** to each of these questions.

1. The **brontosaurus** was a meat eater. ______________
2. The **triceratops** had three horns. ______________
3. The **stegosaurus** had a spiky tail. ______________
4. Your **waist** is part of your leg. ______________
5. **August** comes after **July**. ______________
6. **Autumn** comes after **spring**. ______________
7. Find the correct name and write it under each shape.

kite hexagon octagon pentagon

______________ ______________ ______________ ______________

Activity 17 Name ______________________________

Similar

A **synonym** is a word that means the same or almost the same as another word.

To help you with the work on this page use the list of synonyms on page 180 of the *Collins First School Dictionary*.

1. Find a suitable synonym for each phrase. The first one has been done for you.

a correct reply

a correct answer

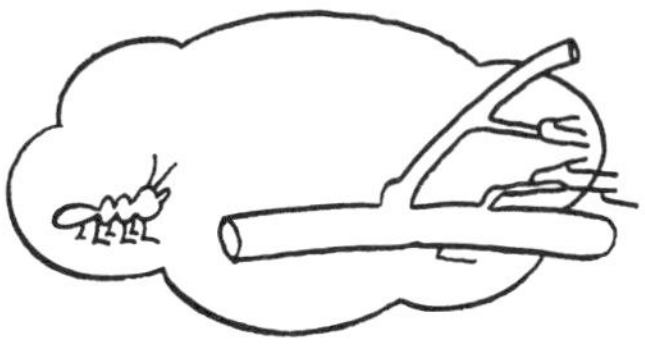

a tiny insect

a __________ insect

a tidy drawer

a __________ drawer

an unhappy girl

a __________ girl

2. Write a word which means the same or almost the same as each of these words.

afraid ______________ fast ______________

yell ______________ cook ______________

Activity 18 Name ______________________

Different

An **antonym** is a word that means the opposite of another word.

To help you with the work on this page use the list of antonyms on page 181 of the *Collins First School Dictionary*.

1. Write an antonym, or opposite, of the words below.

soft ______________	dark ______________
narrow ______________	quiet ______________
few ______________	outside ______________

2. Write the antonyms that describe the pictures below. The first one has been done for you.

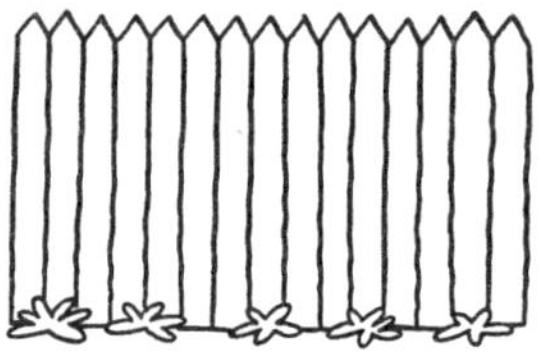

dirty ______ clean ______ ______________ ______________

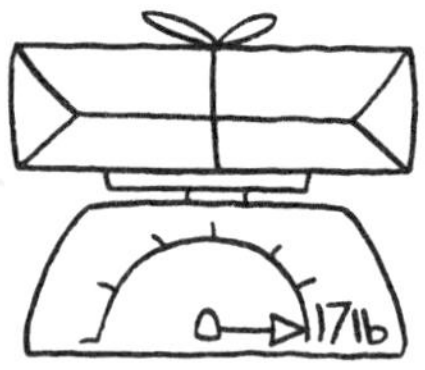

______________ ______________ ______________ ______________

Activity 19

Name ______________________

Find the word (3)

1. Find the word in your dictionary which comes between the two words below:

airport and **alike** ______________

walk and **wand** ______________

star and **start** ______________

famous and **far** ______________

clever and **climb** ______________

trail and **trap** ______________

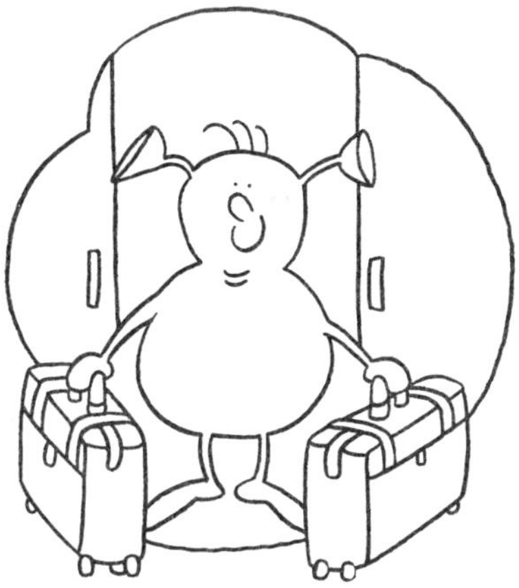

2. Use your dictionary to find these words. Write down the meaning of each one.

few ______________________

stream ______________________

poet ______________________

kettle ______________________

zoo ______________________

Activity 20 Name ______________________________

Find the word (4)

Complete each sentence by finding the correct word in your dictionary and checking its meaning.

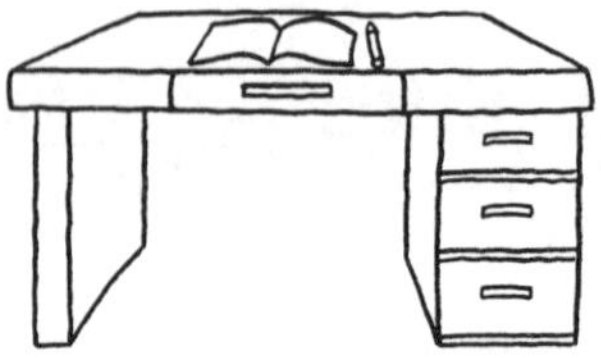

1. A r________ is a small, thick carpet.

2. A c__________ is a young cow or bull.

3. An o___________ is a huge sea.

4. A w___________ is a grown-up female person.

5. S__________ is a white powder that is used to flavour food.

6. When you are ill, you take m________________ to make you better.

7. A d__________ is a special table for working on.

8. A p_____________ is a small nut. It grows in a shell under the ground.

9. W__________ falls from the sky as rain.

10. A k_____________ is a room where food is cooked.

Activity 21 Name ______________________________

Find the meaning

1. Use your dictionary to find the meaning for each word. Draw a line to match each word to its meaning. The first one has been done for you.

	diamond	a vehicle that can travel through space
	pirate	a tiny animal with six legs
	spaceship	a hard bright jewel
	wolf	a sailor who attacks and robs other ships
	insect	a wild animal like a large dog

2. Do the same with these.

	school	a huge, frightening creature
	pen	a hot, dry place
	monster	children go here to learn
	desert	you use this when you write or draw with ink

Activity 22 Name ______________________

More than one meaning

Some words have more than one meaning:

bark
1 The **bark** of a tree is the hard covering of its trunk.
2 A dog that **barks** makes a short, loud sound.

Use your dictionary to find the meaning that matches the picture.

1. match ______________________

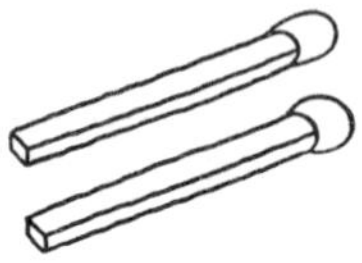

____

2. squash ______________________

____

3. park ______________________

____

4. trip ______________________

____

5. stick ______________________

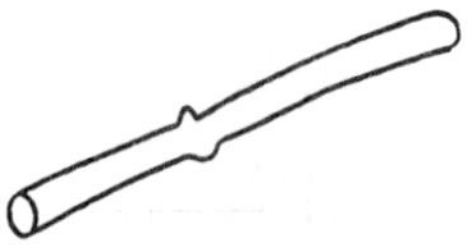

____

Activity 23 Name ______________________

Anagrams

Rearrange the letters to spell the word for each picture. Check the spelling in your dictionary. Write the page number.

pea

____

flow

____

redbag

____

flea

____

sore

____

foal

____

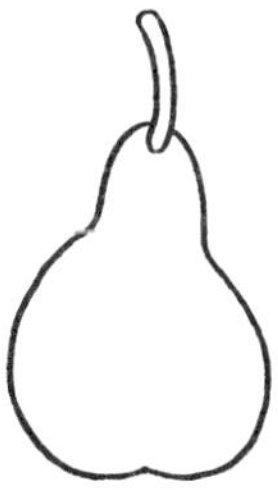
reap

____

cheap

____

cafe

____

Activity 24 Name ____________________

Rhyme time

Words which rhyme often have the same letters at the end.
Write a rhyming word for each word below. Use the picture clues to help you.

pen

____

sing

____

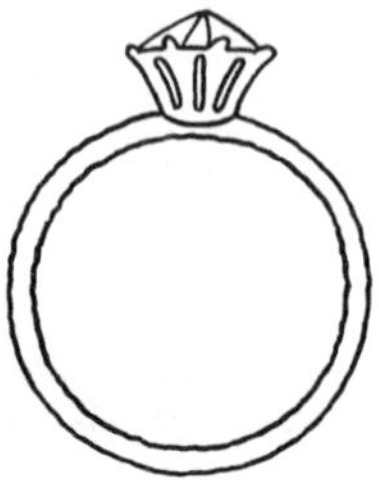

rock

____

top

____

pain

____

sold

____

fair

____

shark

____

Activity 25 Name ____________________

The right spelling (1)

Long a

Put **ai**, **ay** or **a–e** in the spaces below. Check the spellings in your dictionary.

g___t___

pl___ ___

tr___ ___n

Long e

Put **ee** or **ea** in the spaces below. Check the spellings in your dictionary.

l___ ___f

tr___ ___

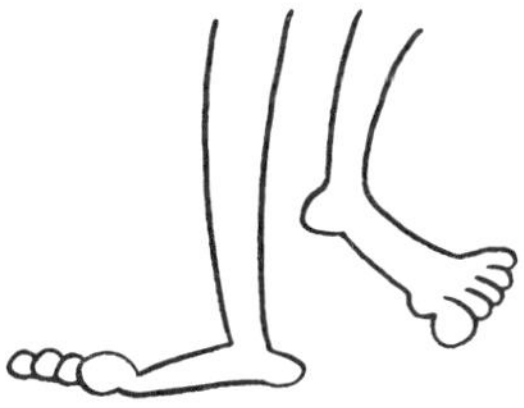

f___ ___t

Long o

Put **oa**, **ow** or **o–e** in the spaces below. Check the spellings in your dictionary.

p___l___

b___ ___t

b___ ___

Activity 26 Name ______________________

The right spelling (2)

Long i

Put **ie**, **i–e**, **igh** or **y** in the spaces below. Check the spellings in your dictionary.

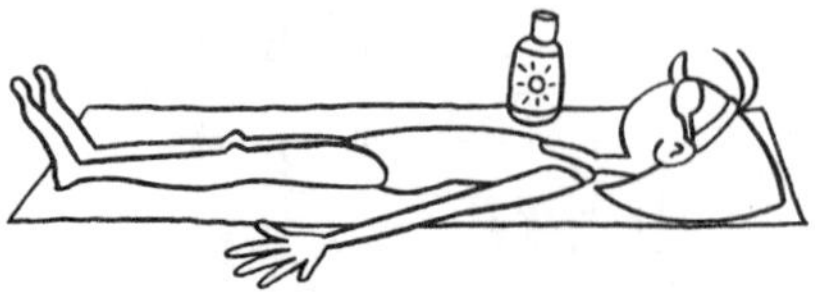

cr___ b___t___ l______

It goes h_________ in the sk___.

Long u

Put **oo**, **u–e**, **ew** or **ue** in the spaces below. Check the spellings in your dictionary.

m______n t___n___ fl______

Use gl______ to stick things together.

Activity 27 Name ____________________

Building words

Sometimes two short words can be put together to make a longer word.

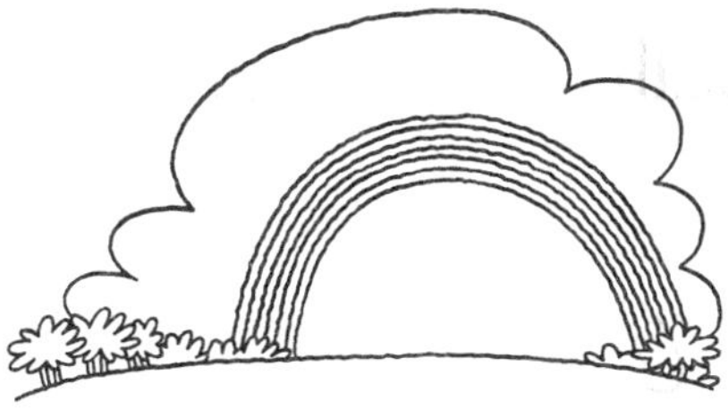

rain + bow = rainbow

1. Make long words from these words.

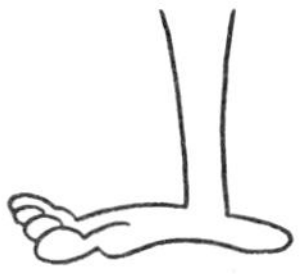
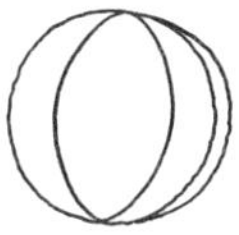

light + house = ____________ foot + ball = ______________

2. Match up these short words to make longer words.

class	board
black	storm
door	brush
motor	room
play	paper
tooth	fly
thunder	bike
news	ground
butter	bell

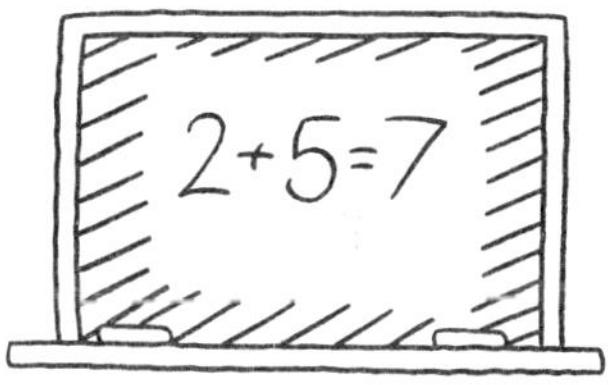

Activity 28 Name ______________________

More than one

Singular means <u>one</u> person or thing.
Plural means <u>more than one</u>.

One **cat**

Three **cats**

One **dragon**

Two **dragons**

When you look up the word for something, your dictionary gives you the singular and plural of it. Look up the word **bucket**. Right after **bucket** is its plural, **buckets**.

1. Use your dictionary to find the plural of these words.

duck ______________________ mountain ______________________

bush ______________________ shelf ______________________

baby ______________________ potato ______________________

2. Do the same with these.

house ______________________ strawberry ______________________

leaf ______________________ branch ______________________

Activity 29 Name ______________________

Verbs

Verbs are words that say what is happening or being done.

Verbs have different forms.

I jump. She jump**s**. He is jump**ing**. We jump**ed**.

Your dictionary gives all these different forms.

Write the different forms for the verbs below.
The first one has been done for you.

1. smile ___smiles___ ___smiling___ ___smiled___
2. bury ______ ______ ______
3. walk ______ ______ ______
4. carry ______ ______ ______
5. laugh ______ ______ ______
6. cry ______ ______ ______
7. hurry ______ ______ ______
8. dive ______ ______ ______
9. slip ______ ______ ______
10. bark ______ ______ ______

Activity 30 Name ____________________

Sounds similar (1)

In some words the same sound is spelled differently.

The clown blew the trumpet loudly.

Use your dictionary to find the correct spelling for these words.

ow and ou

cl_____d cr_____d sh_____t

oi and oy

b_____l t_____ c_____n

oo and u

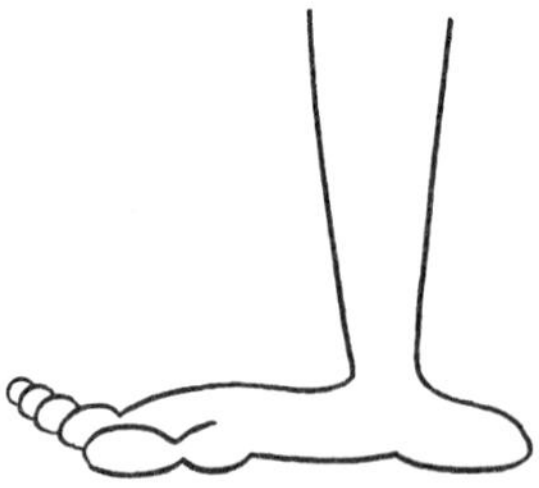

b__________ p__________ f__________

Activity 31

Name ____________________

Sounds similar (2)

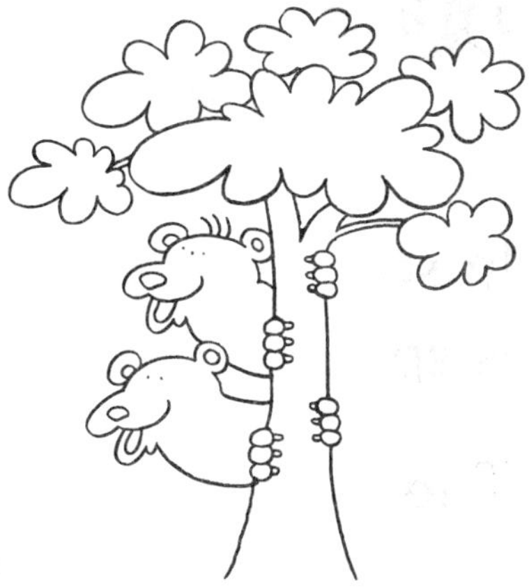

All these words have the same sound, but are spelled differently.

A pair of bears gave Tom a scare over there.

Complete these words with the correct spelling: **air**, **ear**, **are** or **ere**. Check your answer in a dictionary.

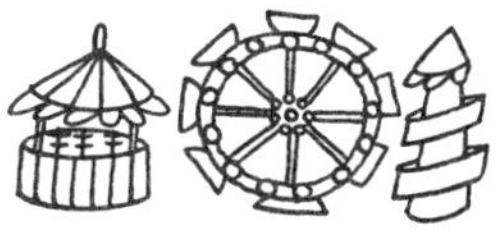  

f________ p________ sh________

Did you te______ this dress?

It is rude to st________.

Her h________ was very long.

Take c________. The st________s are steep.

Wh________ will you w________ that hat?

Activity 32 Name ______________________________

Look, Say, Cover, Write, Check

Use the Look, Say, Cover, Write, Check method to learn how to spell difficult words.

Look **Say** **Cover** **Write** **Check**

If you spell the word wrong, use Look, Say, Cover, Write, Check to try again.

Look, Say, Cover	Write	Check	Try again	Check
difficult	dificult	✗	difficult	✓

Activity 33 Name ______________________________

Word fun

Read the clues and use your dictionary to help you complete this crossword.

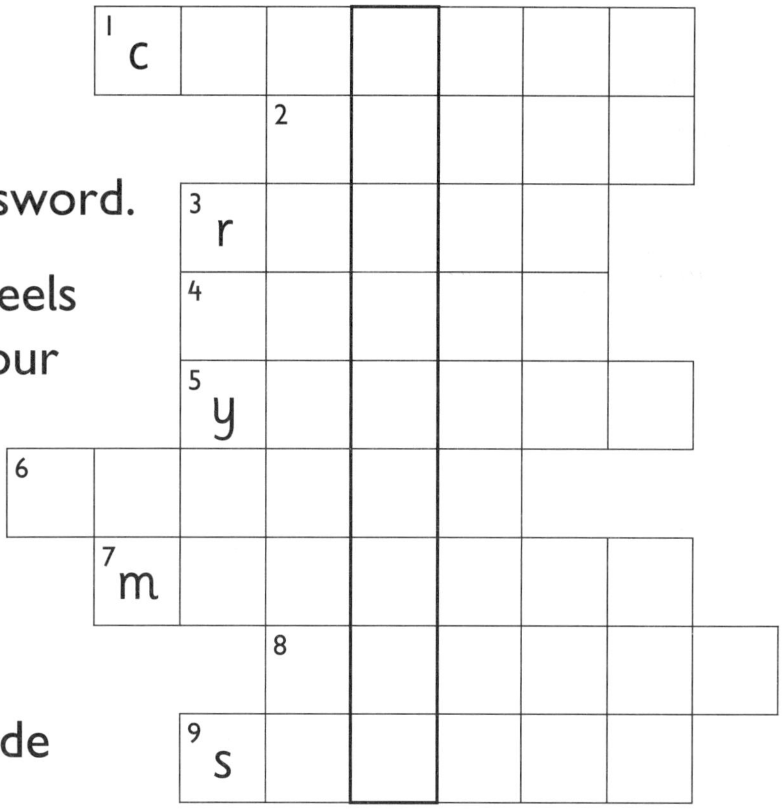

1. a small house on wheels
2. the middle part of your arm which bends
3. used for measuring or for drawing straight lines
4. two times
5. a soft, thick food made from milk
6. the day of the week between Thursday and Saturday
7. something that is wrong
8. something is this if it wobbles
9. a person who is this can lift heavy things

What animal's name can you find? ____________________

Alphabet code

Write the words in alphabetical order to read the message.

tomorrow for Zoe drinks picnic our Bring

____

______________________________________ . ____________

Activity 34

Name ____________________

Word search

The names of eight animals are hidden in this word search. Find them and write their names. Use the picture clues and your dictionary to help you.

a	c	o	t	t	e	r	t
l	h	a	m	s	t	e	r
t	i	g	e	p	p	i	g
n	m	y	r	j	f	w	r
p	p	i	n	c	d	s	l
r	a	b	b	i	t	y	h
f	n	l	g	u	m	v	o
o	z	x	d	a	a	d	r
x	e	y	c	a	e	r	s
z	e	b	r	a	m	s	e

____________________ ____________________ ____________________

____________________ ____________________ ____________________

____________________ ____________________

Activity 35

Name ______________________________

Musical instruments

1. What are the names of these musical instruments? Check the spellings in your dictionary.

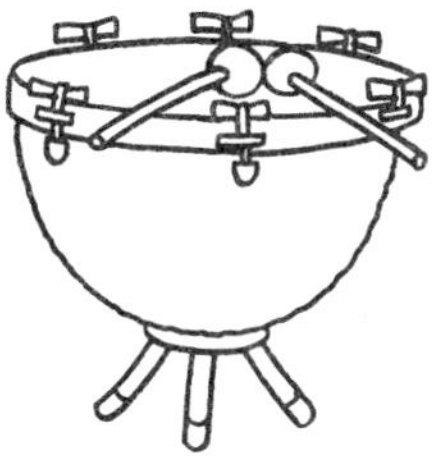

d ____ ____ ____

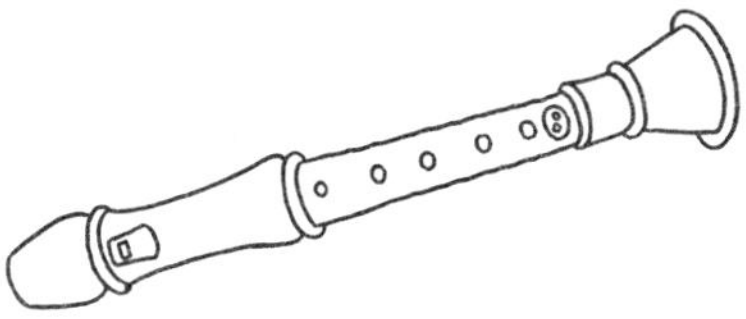

v ____ ____ ____ ____ ____

r ____ ____ ____ ____ ____ ____ ____

p ____ ____ ____ ____

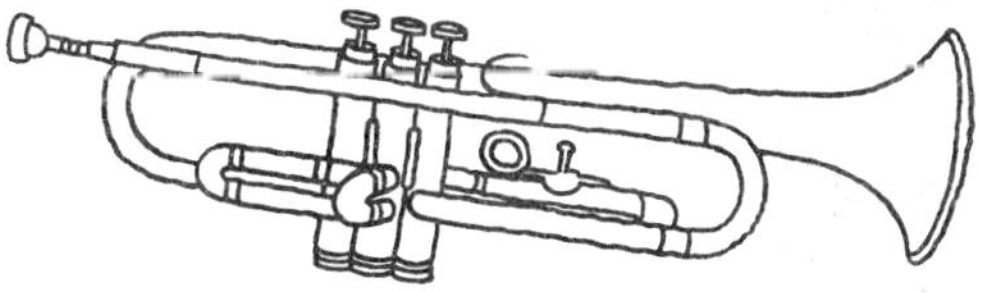

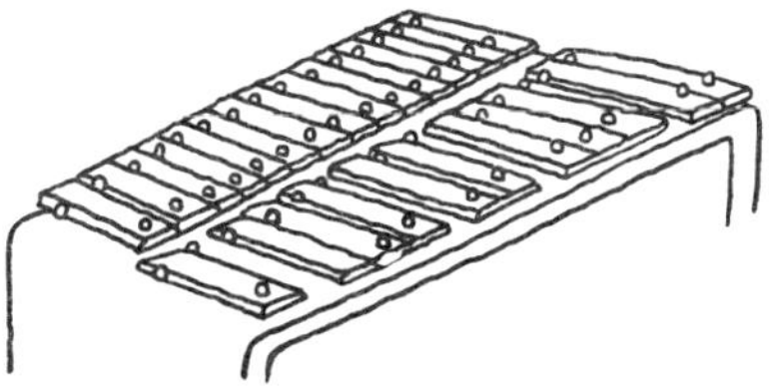

t ____ ____ ____ ____ ____ ____

x ____ ____ ____ ____ ____ ____ ____ ____

g ____ ____ ____ ____ ____

2. What is the name of a large group of people who play music together?

o ____ ____ ____ ____ ____ ____ ____ ____

Activity 36 Name ______________________

Word steps

Read the clues and use your dictionary to help you complete these word steps.

Clues

1 a pain that goes on hurting
2 a sound that you make comes back to you
3 a flat shape with a curved edge, like the shape of an egg
4 bend in one direction
5 information about things that have just happened
6 breathe out slowly and make a sad sound
7 a man or boy who has done something brave or good
8 to do what someone says
9 belonging to you
10 a deep, loud noise like a lion makes
11 not seen very often

Activity 37 Name ______

Quiz time (1)

Use your dictionary to find these words.

a large group of soldiers **a**______

a vehicle that travels across water **b**______

a baby bird **c**______

a large metal or plastic container for rubbish **d**______

a green jewel **e**______

the second month of the year **F**______

a kind of door in a fence or wall **g**______

a sweet, sticky food made by bees **h**______

a strong, hard, grey metal **i**______

a container for holding liquids **j**______

a toy that you fly in the air **k**______

a young sheep **l**______

a kind of jam, usually made from oranges **m**______

Activity 38 Name ______________________

Quiz time (2)

Use your dictionary to find these words.

the time when it is dark **n**__________

a white vegetable with a strong taste **o**__________

a small, round stone **p**__________

the cry of a duck **q**__________

things that you throw away **r**__________

somewhere that you sit **s**__________

an animal like a large frog **t**__________

the brother of your mother or father **u**__________

someone who looks after sick animals **v**__________

the person who wins something **w**__________

a photograph of the inside of your body **X**__________

the yellow part in the middle of an egg **y**__________

a line that bends suddenly up and down **z**__________

Activity 39 Name ____________________

Making a word bank

A word bank is a collection of interesting words on a particular topic.
Put the words below into their correct word bank. Use your dictionary to find more words for each word bank.

March wrist trousers windscreen knee

bumper tie Sunday year afternoon headlight

blouse elbow trainers engine morning

Clothes

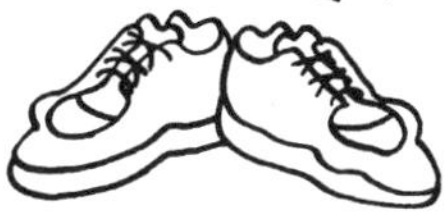

Time words

Parts of the body

Parts of a car

Activity 40 Name ______________________________

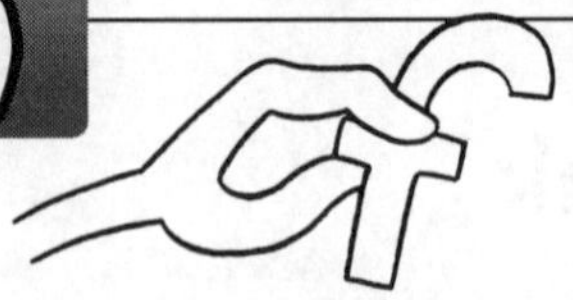

Collecting words

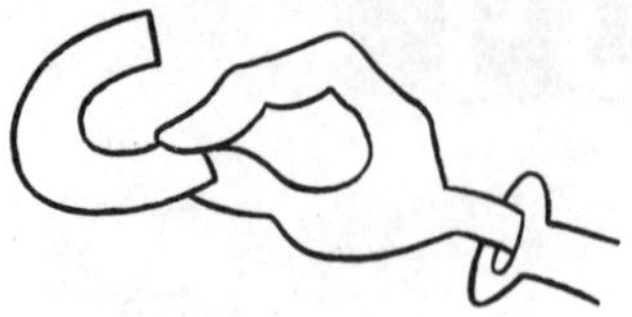

Use this sheet to make your own collection of words. Here are some ideas for a word collection:

- words connected with a topic you are interested in
- words you want to learn to spell
- words you have learned to spell
- your favourite words

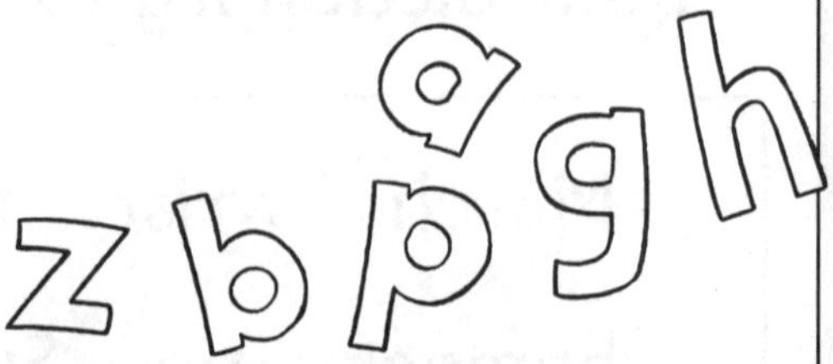

Make sure you know the meaning of the words you collect. Use the Look, Say, Cover, Write, Check way to learn how to spell them.

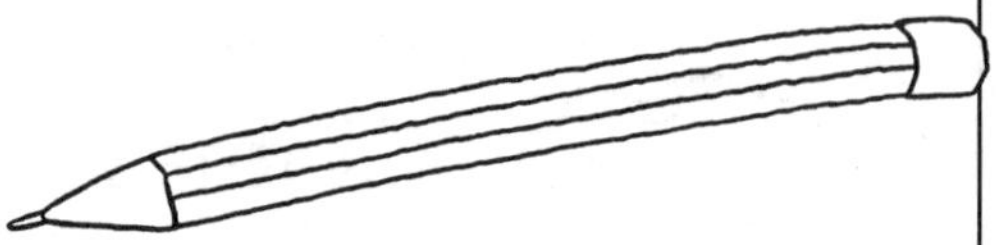

<u>Word</u> <u>Definition</u>

______________________ ______________________________________

____

______________________ ______________________________________

____

______________________ ______________________________________

____

______________________ ______________________________________

____